TWENTIETH CENTURY TRAILBLAZERS

CONTENTS

1 100 years of change	2
2 Children's authors	8
3 Painters	16
4 Architects	24
5 Singers	32
6 Photographers	40
7 Composers	48
8 Classical musicians	56
9 Fashion designers	64
10 What next?	74
Glossary	76
Index	77
100 years	78

Written by Zoë Clarke

Collins

1 100 YEARS OF CHANGE

At the start of the 20th century, women and girls in some parts of the world had little or no rights. In the UK, working-class women and girls worked long hours in low-paid jobs as domestic servants, or in textile factories. An unmarried middle-class woman who wanted paid work didn't have much choice. She could become a governess or a music teacher – possibly a nurse. All women were expected to get married, look after the home and have a family.

The suffragette movement campaigned to change the rules governing what women could and couldn't do. They wanted women to have the right to vote and they used lots of different methods to persuade people to give them what they wanted. Their motto was "Deeds not words" – they wanted people to stop talking about change and start *doing* things to change how women were treated. The suffragettes had some success, but it was war that changed the roles of women forever.

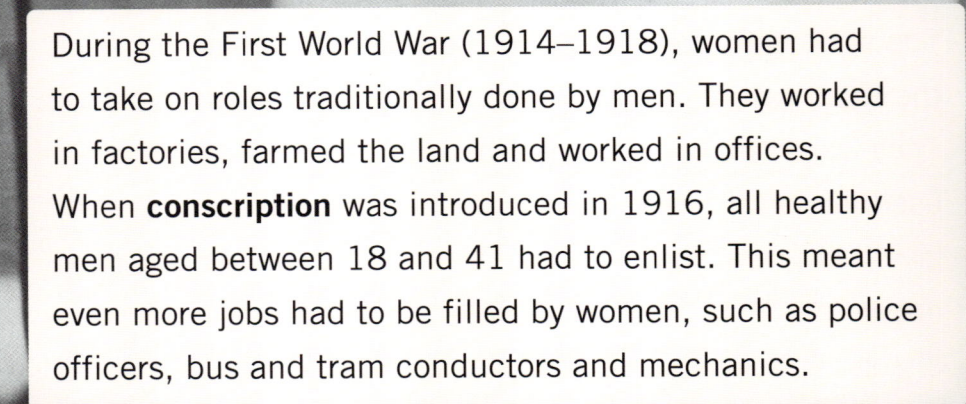

During the First World War (1914–1918), women had to take on roles traditionally done by men. They worked in factories, farmed the land and worked in offices. When **conscription** was introduced in 1916, all healthy men aged between 18 and 41 had to enlist. This meant even more jobs had to be filled by women, such as police officers, bus and tram conductors and mechanics.

About five million women did war work during the First World War.

No one could ignore the contribution women had made during the war, but soldiers returning from the front lines were given their old jobs back. However, there was some good news for women. In 1918, women over 30 who owned property were allowed to vote, and by 1928, women over the age of 21 were allowed to vote, just like men.

During the Second World War (1939–1945), women once again filled the jobs usually done by men. In 1941, over 640,000 single women aged 20–30 were conscripted to work in the armed forces, but not in fighting roles. Many women also worked near the front lines as nurses or driving ambulances.

nighttime training for female ambulance drivers

Despite all their war work, for women, the early 1950s looked very much like the first half of the century. Girls leaving school were still expected to get married and look after the home, but in the 1960s things really started to change. More training and educational opportunities became available for young girls leaving school and by 1962 over 26,000 young women were at university.

Other things changed too: skirts got shorter, new music like rock and roll, pop, soul, and rhythm and blues was on the radio, and the "pixie" cut was a bold new hairstyle for women and girls. Young people were inspired by these new ideas.

mini-dress inspired by a football strip, designed by Mary Quant

The Supremes' rhythm and blues music was the sound of the 60s.

the pixie cut

By the 1970s, women had the right to be paid as much as men for doing the same job, and employers were not allowed to **discriminate** against a woman if she was married. In 1979, Margaret Thatcher became the UK's first female Prime Minister, and as the 1980s and 1990s arrived, there were very few jobs women couldn't legally do.

Stella Rimington: first female director of MI5 (1992)

Pauline Clare: first female chief constable in Britain (1995)

Diane Abbott: first Black female Member of Parliament in the UK (1987)

2 CHILDREN'S AUTHORS

For much of the 20th century, publishing houses were run by men, but there were female authors, illustrators, editors and librarians behind the scenes. They were known as "bookwomen".

The Tale of Peter Rabbit, by Beatrix Potter, was published in 1902 and many stories written by women featuring animals followed: runaway animals, magical animals, and smart animals, like the dogs in *The Hundred and One Dalmatians* by Dodie Smith (1956).

Fiction aimed at girls became popular, particularly boarding school stories. Strong female characters in Elinor M Brent-Dyer's Chalet School series confront real-life events: *The Chalet School in Exile* (1940), follows the school as it moves from Austria after the Germans invade during the Second World War.

Women writers were creating interesting, intelligent characters. Catherine Storr's smart heroine in *Clever Polly and the Stupid Wolf* (1955) and courageous Bonnie Green in Joan Aiken's *The Wolves of Willoughby Chase* (1962) are bold and resourceful. They're girls who can solve problems, defeat the villain *and* avoid being eaten. Young readers who liked fantasy stories also had lots of choice: writers like Ursula K Le Guin, Susan Cooper and Diana Wynne Jones wrote about fantastical made-up places in faraway lands.

Authors started writing about real life too: stories set in the past, family stories and stories about how people are treated by others.

At the end of the century, there were lots of new female voices, creating picture books and fiction with strong, female characters, ready to take on the next century.

In Beverley Naidoo's *Journey to Jo'burg* (1985), Naledi and Tiro live in South Africa at a time where there were laws discriminating against Black people because of the colour of their skin.

TOVE JANSSON

Step back in time to 1914, the year writer and artist Tove Jansson was born. Tove and her two brothers, Lars and Per, grew up in a household full of inspiring, creative people. Their mother, Signe, was an illustrator and graphic designer and their father, Viktor, was a sculptor. The family lived in a tiny apartment in Helsinki, Finland, which was both a home and an artists' studio. Tove's parents painted the walls, ceilings and floors; there was artwork on the walls by family friends, shelves heaving with books and Viktor's sculptures.

Tove was hugely influenced by her parents' artistic lifestyle, and by the time she was seven, she had started to write her own stories and illustrate them. By 16, Tove had published her first story.

In 1930, when she was 16, Tove moved from Helsinki to Stockholm. She went to lots of different art schools, and studied ceramic art, painting and drawing. Tove also studied in Paris, and in 1944 she set up her own studio back in Helsinki, earning a living painting and illustrating. It was easier to make money from illustrating, and for over 20 years, Tove drew cartoons for a magazine called *Garm*. During the Second World War, Tove's cartoons made fun of the enemy, which was brave and dangerous.

Unlike many women at that time, Tove didn't "settle down" and get married. Tove met her partner, Tuulikki Pietilä, in 1955. Tuulikki, known as "Tooti", was a graphic artist; Tooti and Tove worked from separate apartments in the same building.

THE MOOMINS

In 1945, Tove had a book published, and it was something different from everything else. *The Moomins and the Great Flood* was written and illustrated while the Second World War was still happening; many families were separated during the war, and Tove wanted to write about this. But instead of writing about a human family, Tove invented some brand-new creatures, called Moomins.

Tove wrote lots of books about the Moomins.

In the Moomin world, everyone can be part of the family and live in Moominvalley. Moomintroll, Moominmamma and Moominpapa are joined by lots of different kinds of creatures including Sniff, Snorkmaiden, Snork, Hemulen, Little My, Too-Ticky, Toffle, Fillyjonks, Mymble, and Moomintroll's best friend, Snufkin. Everyone looks different, but everyone's welcome as a new friend. There's snow, fierce rain and flooding but everyone tries to do good things and care for others. This was the opposite of the way people had been treated during the war.

In 1954, a Moomin cartoon strip drawn by Tove was published in the British newspaper *The Evening News*. 20 million readers saw the Moomins, and they wanted more! The Moomins become world famous, but after five years, Tove didn't want to keep drawing the cartoons, and her brother Lars took over.

Moomins also appeared on postage stamps.

ISLAND LIFE

Tove and Tooti spent lots of time on the Finnish islands of Bredskär, and Klovharu. Klovharu is a tiny, rocky place, and Tove and Tooti spent many summers there. There was no electricity or running water and they camped in a tent while they built a one-bedroom hut. They had desks in the hut to work from, and Tove wrote some of the Moomin books while she was there. Days were spent chopping wood, making fires and fishing. This wasn't the kind of behaviour expected from two women, but Tove and Tooti did it anyway.

Tove standing in front of the house on Klovharu island

MOOMINS FOREVER

Tove's last Moomin novel, *Moominvalley in November*, was published in 1970. But that wasn't the end for the Moomins. There was a Moomin opera and a Moomin television show; Moomin plays are still performed around the world. In 1986, Tove donated her Moomin artwork to the Tampere Museum. In 2017 the work was moved to a dedicated Moomin museum, and in 1993, Moominworld opened on a small island in Finland. Thousands of people visit every year; Moomin bravery, friendship and love of nature is as relevant today as when the books were first written.

the Moomin house at Moomin World

3 PAINTERS

In the 20th century, there was a revolution in art. Painters didn't want to follow the styles of artists who had come before, they wanted to create something different. The world was changing, and women artists had something to say!

Before the First World War, Expressionism was popular, where painters used bold colours and loose brushstrokes. Cubism followed, where objects are turned into geometric cube-like shapes in bold colours. After the First World War, some painters followed a style called Surrealism; some paintings had misshapen objects that looked like they were melting.

Cubism

16

After the Second World War, painting styles changed again. Abstract Expressionism started in New York, and it was easy to spot! Paintings had forceful brushstrokes and used bold pops of colour. The 1950s and 1960s were all about Pop Art; artists were inspired by comic books, magazines and colour television, which was first broadcast in the UK in 1967. This was followed by Minimalism, where painters used geometric shapes and muted colours.

Abstract Expressionism

Not all artists followed styles or trends – some produced work that was instinctive and expressive, and rooted in the place they lived.

EMILY KAM KNGWARRAY

Emily Kam Kngwarray, also spelt Emily Kame Kngwarreye, is one of Australia's most important **contemporary** artists. Born in Alhalkere, around 1910, Emily was a member of the Anmatyerre people – Aboriginal people of Northern Territory.

In the 1920s, the first White people colonised the region near Alhalkere, and gave the lands shared by five major **ancestral groups** the name Utopia. The colonisers set up **homesteads** and large farms called cattle stations.

Emily was a **domestic worker** at several different farms; she also herded cattle, which was unusual for a woman in the 1930s.

In 1977, Emily, along with other women from her community, was taught how to make batik fabric as part of an educational programme. She was a founding member of the Utopia Women's Batik Group: the women applied hot wax designs to fabric, placed the fabric into containers of dye, then removed the wax with hot water to reveal the pattern.

By 1988–1989, when Emily was in her late 70s, she started to work with acrylic paint on canvas. Emily used some of the skills she'd learnt when making batik fabric in her approach to painting; she liked painting because it was much quicker than creating batik patterns.

Emily working on one of her paintings

CONNECTION TO THE LAND

Emily was an Anmatyerre Elder and a ceremonial leader belonging to the Anmatyerre people. As part of the women's ceremony, called "Alwelye", women paint traditional patterns on their skin with a powder made from charcoal, **ochre** and ash. This tradition is thousands of years old; dots, geometrical patterns and images, including plants and animals, are applied with a flat stick or fingers. The women also speak, chant, dance, use hand gestures and tell their stories to connect with the land.

The ancestor rock, Alhalkere, is a **sacred** place for the Anmatyerre people.
As an Elder, Emily protected sites like this.

Painting geometrical patterns on rocks, and creating patterns and images on the ground using different coloured sand, is also part of this unique tradition of storytelling. The patterns and images record the past, mark territory and they're sacred to First Australians. Emily used this knowledge when she started painting on canvas.

Patterns and shapes in the sand are made using a finger or a pointed stick.

CREATING A PAINTING

People, animals, objects and places are represented by colours, lines, shapes and different textures. Emily used brushes, sticks and her fingers to make marks and her method of painting is known as "dub dub" – the name comes from the sound of a brush, heavy with paint, as it hits the canvas.

Layers of paint, flowing brushwork and crisscrossing coloured lines were used to create this painting. Many of her paintings use deep red, orange and pink – desert colours.

This painting has been created with layers of coloured dots and fan-shaped dabs of paint.

PRESERVING THE PAST, FOR THE FUTURE

In 1989, the work made by women artists in the Utopia area was shown in an art exhibition in Sydney. Emily's first painting, *Emu Woman* (1988–1989), was used on the catalogue cover for the exhibition, and when people saw her work, they wanted to buy it. Emily, and her art, was suddenly famous. In 1990, Emily had her first solo exhibition, and in 1992, she was awarded an Australian Creative Arts Fellowship – the first time a First Australian artist had ever received such an award.

Emily went on to produce over 3,000 paintings in eight years – an average of one painting a day – and exhibitions of her work have since been put on all around the world. Each painting is the story of her life as an Anmatyerre woman, a response to traditions she upheld and her connection to the land where she was born.

4 ARCHITECTS

Architects design buildings and spaces around them.

If you wanted to be an architect at the start of the 20th century, there weren't many places to study if you were a woman, but after the First and Second World Wars, there were fewer male students. This meant more places for women at the Architectural Association School of Architecture and the Royal Institute of British Architects (RIBA) in London.

There's an architect for every type of building and space. Women wanted to prove that they could design buildings too.

Residential architects design new houses.

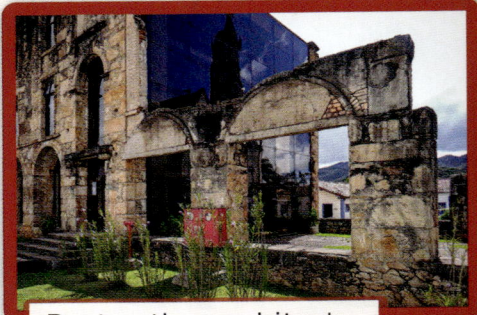

Restoration architects **preserve** old buildings.

Green architects design eco-friendly buildings.

With the turn of the century, there were lots of new ideas about how buildings should be designed. In the 1920s and 1930s, Art Deco was a popular style in the UK, Europe and the USA. Architects used bold geometric shapes with curved walls and windows.

From the 1930s to the early 1960s, a different style of architecture had arrived – Modernism. No more curves or detailed designs, these buildings had little or no decoration and were constructed using lots of glass, steel and concrete. What a building was used for became the most important thing, rather than how it looked.

Not every Modernist building looks like this. One architect took the idea of Modernism, reimagined it, and created her own unique style.

ZAHA HADID

Zaha Hadid was an award-winning Iraqi-British architect. Her futuristic, **groundbreaking** steel, glass and concrete designs can be found in cities and towns around the world.

This is the Riverside Museum of transport and technology, in Glasgow, UK, which Zaha and her team designed. The museum is next to the river Clyde, and the angular, wave-like shape of the roof was designed to link the city to the waterfront and highlight Glasgow's shipbuilding history.

Zaha was born in 1950, in Baghdad, Iraq. Her father, Mohammed, was a politician and her mother, Wajeeha, was an artist. When Zaha was about six years old, a family friend who was an architect brought some drawings and small-scale models of buildings to show them. Zaha remembered being interested in the small models.

Samarra

Later, when she was at school, a teacher took Zaha's class to visit a museum in Baghdad. They were allowed into the storage area, where she saw thousands of glass cases full of objects. Zaha was amazed by these hidden treasures!

The family often travelled to towns and cities in southern Iraq — day trips with picnics to the ruins of Samarra — and abroad. In Córdoba, Spain, Zaha visited the Great Mosque and she saw that old buildings could also look very modern. All these childhood experiences influenced the kind of architect Zaha was to become.

BECOMING AN ARCHITECT

Zaha studied mathematics at the American University of Beirut, Lebanon. In 1972, she moved to London and studied at the Architectural Association School of Architecture; when she graduated in 1977, Zaha won the prize for best student.

In 1979, Zaha opened her own architectural firm, Zaha Hadid Architects, but for years no one wanted to build the kind of structures she was designing; they were seen as too expensive, too complicated and too ambitious. Zaha didn't change the way she worked, she waited for the right client to say "Yes!" and that's what happened.

This angular, grey concrete building was built between 1991 and 1993. It was commissioned by the director of a company called Vitra, in Weil am Rhein, Germany.

28

Today, the building is used for events and exhibitions, but it was originally designed as a fire station. There's space for a team of firefighters, and the fire engines, wrapped up in Zaha's **cutting-edge** design. Zaha said the Vitra Fire Station was one of her favourite buildings. It's been described as a "frozen explosion" because of its striking concrete spikes and angles.

In 1999, Zaha and her team designed a new ski jump in Innsbruck, Austria. The monumental structure, with its sweeping curves, is 50 metres tall and sits between the mountain slopes. The tower is made of concrete and there's a café at the top, with wide glass windows.

THE 20TH CENTURY ... AND BEYOND!

Zaha became the first woman to win the important Pritzker Architecture Prize, in 2004, for her design for the Contemporary Arts Center, Cincinnati, USA, and more building commissions and awards followed.

The Heydar Aliyev Cultural Center, Azerbaijan, was completed in 2012. Sweeping curves made from reinforced concrete and steel were covered with panels of fibreglass reinforced with polyester and more concrete!

Port House, Antwerp, Belgium, was completed in 2016. A disused fire station was renovated, and a brand-new diamond-shaped structure covered in glass was added to the top. The new building looks like the hull of a ship.

Zaha has been called the most famous female architect in the world, and her building designs have won lots of prizes. Zaha's designs continue to inspire others, and her team of architects continue her extraordinary work.

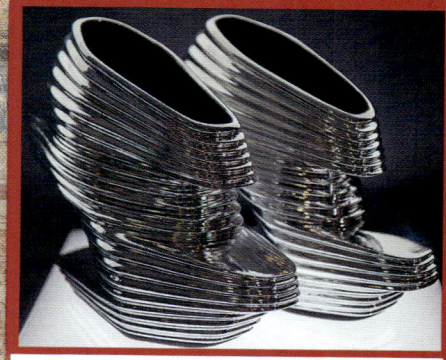

Zaha also designed jewellery, furniture and shoes!

5 SINGERS

If you wanted to hear a performance by a classical or operatic singer in the early 20th century, you might have gone to a concert hall. Microphones hadn't been invented, so singers belted out their songs as loudly as they could so everyone could hear them. Then microphones were developed; singers could perform naturally, because they didn't have to shout.

New sounds included "crooning" – songs sung in a quiet, low tone, like a lullaby. Then came jazz and the best and brightest jazz singers were women. Americans Ella Fitzgerald, Nina Simone and Billie Holiday were successful because their voices were powerful and showed emotion. More people started to own radios – with the turn of a dial, everyone had music transmitted directly into their home.

Ella Fitzgerald

Rock and roll arrived in the 1950s and never went away. The 1970s was disco time! It had lots of repeated phrases and catchy choruses; words were easy to learn and sing along to. Disco was replaced by electronic dance music in the 1980s; singers do feature on some of this music, but the sound was more important than words.

By the 1970s, Joan Jett was known as "the queen of rock and roll".

At the end of the 20th century, music from around the globe was being played on the radio; singers and songwriters were making vibrant, original sounds.

MIRIAM MAKEBA

Miriam Makeba was a dynamic singer and a performer whose voice made her internationally famous; a woman who used her platform to speak up for what she believed in, stepping into a role that earned her the name "Mama Africa".

Miriam was born in 1932. She was the youngest of five children, and her family lived in Prospect Township, just outside Johannesburg, South Africa. Her father, Caswell, was a clerk for the oil company Shell, and her mother, Christina, was a domestic worker. Miriam loved to sing from a very young age; she sang when she was at school, and she sang when she was at church. But singing wasn't a job Miriam could get paid for at first. Miriam's father died when she was a young child; the family needed money and as soon as she was old enough, Miriam helped her mother clean houses.

LIVING UNDER APARTHEID

In 1948, when Miriam was 16, the government of South Africa introduced apartheid. This was a law that said that Black and mixed-race people had to live in different areas from White people, and use separate public facilities, such as schools. In the 20 years that followed, more than three and a half million Black and mixed-race people were forced to relocate into areas with poorly-built houses that had no running water or electricity.

These homes were for Black and mixed-race people. They didn't own the houses or the land.

These homes were for White people. They could own their own houses and land.

SOPHIATOWN

In the 1950s, Miriam lived in Sophiatown. It was a crowded, vibrant place with a diverse mix of people from different backgrounds. There were theatres, showing American films, and lots of dance parties. It was home to many different music sounds, including African Jazz.

The South African government didn't want people from different cultures to live together in Sophiatown. It was also very close to an area where White people lived, and the government didn't like that either. In 1955, everyone living in Sophiatown was forced to move to a new area; by 1960, Sophiatown had been demolished.

At that time, over 60,000 people lived in Sophiatown.

MOVING ON

In the 1950s, Miriam started singing with two all-male groups: The Cuban Brothers and The Manhattan Brothers. She also joined an all-female group called The Skylarks. Miriam was getting paid, and she sang in different African languages: Xhosa (the language Miriam spoke as a child), Sotho, Zulu and Swahili. She also sang in English, long before she could speak it.

In 1959, Miriam had a small part in a film called *Come Back, Africa*. The American director made the film in secret, and smuggled the material out of South Africa, because the film criticised the South African government and their apartheid laws. At that time, it was difficult for Black artists to leave South Africa, but Miriam *did* get away, first to the UK and then to the USA. The South African government didn't like the film, and they didn't like Miriam's success. In response, they cancelled her passport, so she was unable to visit her family in South Africa. Later, other countries offered Miriam a passport, which meant she was able to travel.

ACTIVIST

Miriam couldn't go home, so she focused on her singing. In New York in 1959, Miriam appeared on a popular television show and 60 million people around the world got to hear her sing. No one in South Africa was able to listen because the government had banned her songs.

One of Miriam's songs, "The Click Song", used sounds taken from the Zulu languages. It was a new kind of music for audiences outside South Africa, and it was a hit. But it was the upbeat rhythm of another song, "Pata Pata", that made people want to get up and dance! It got to number 12 on the USA Billboard music charts in 1967, the first South African record to do so. Miriam added English lyrics to the song, and it remains one of her most popular.

When Miriam was in New York, she sang at the Apollo Theatre.

Miriam never forgot about South Africa, and many of her songs had protest messages. In 1963, Miriam gave a speech at the **United Nations**, in New York, which had set up a special committee to gather information about what was happening in South Africa. It was unusual for a woman to give a speech like this, but she was determined to stand up and fight for what she believed in: freedom of speech, freedom of movement and the right to be treated equally and fairly. Miriam became one of the most well-known and outspoken critics of the apartheid laws. In response, the South African government took away Miriam's citizenship. With no citizenship, Miriam couldn't live in South Africa, and she remained in **exile** for 30 years.

Miriam returned to South Africa in 1990, when the apartheid system started to collapse. By that time, she'd recorded hundreds of songs, won awards, and become well-known around the world. Miriam had a voice people listened to, whether she was singing or speaking up for others. For Miriam, "music was a type of magic" – it was the kind of magic that changed her life, and those around her.

6 PHOTOGRAPHERS

In 1900, an American company called Kodak started selling a camera called the Brownie. You didn't have to be a professional photographer to use a Brownie or have lots of money to buy one. Anyone could take black-and-white photographs of anything they wanted, and the camera cost five shillings (25 pence).

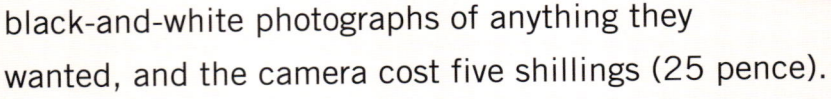

For professional photographers, taking formal portraits was a good way to make a living, but change was on its way. Photographers wanted to document "real" things: people's lives, what was happening in society … and war. Lee Miller was the first female photojournalist to work near the front lines during the Second World War.

Margaret Bourke-White worked with the USA armed forces during the Second World War.

Today, if you have a mobile phone, you can take a photograph with a click of a button, but it was only in the 1960s and 1970s that it was possible to take a colour photograph.

As cameras got better, different photographic styles emerged, and some professional photographers focused on one area: people, wildlife or landscapes. Others used specific methods, such as macro photography (zooming in very close to something) or astro photography (zooming out wide to capture the night sky).

Pioneering female photographers in the early part of the 20th century used photographs to document real-life events and laid the foundation for more women to tell their own stories.

DOROTHEA LANGE

Dorothea Lange was born in 1895, New Jersey, USA, five years before the first Brownie camera went on sale. When Dorothea was seven, she contracted polio. Today, children are **immunised** against the virus, but Dorothea wasn't so fortunate. There's no cure for polio, and one of the symptoms is a weakness in your muscles that can lead to **paralysis**. Dorothea's right leg and foot were affected, and she walked with a limp for the rest of her life.

When she was at high school, Dorothea spent lots of time in the school library, looking at photography books, and decided she was going to be a photographer. But Dorothea's mother enrolled her at the New York Training School for Teachers, because women could get jobs in schools. Dorothea didn't stay there long; instead she worked at a photo studio in New York, and then studied photography at Columbia University.

In 1918, Dorothea planned to travel around the world with a friend, but when she got to San Francisco, California, someone stole her money. She decided to stay in the city and got a job working for a shop called Marsh and Company that sold photographic equipment. A year later, Dorothea set up her own portrait studio and even carried on working after she got married in 1920. This was unusual for a woman, but Dorothea liked working with people and she was very good at her job.

San Francisco in the 1920s

THE GREAT DEPRESSION

From 1929 to 1941, the USA suffered the Great Depression. Millions of people were out of work and families lost their homes because they didn't have any money to pay for them. Many people didn't have enough food to eat. Then, in 1931–1932, there was a drought. The southern Great Plains (an area covering the states of Colorado, Kansas, Oklahoma, New Mexico and Texas) were so dry the area was called the Dust Bowl, and farmers couldn't grow enough crops to sell. Thousands of people migrated west, hoping to find work.

Dorothea saw people on the streets of San Francisco who had migrated to the area, many of whom were homeless, and she started to photograph them. This was a new style of photography for Dorothea, and she decided to close her studio and photograph the changes that were happening in society. In 1935, Dorothea was employed by a government agency as a field photographer; she travelled out of the city and took pictures of what was happening to people as they were migrating. This job gave Dorothea the opportunity to capture the impact of the Great Depression.

45

RECORDING THE TRUTH

Dorothea was one of the first women who could be described as a documentary photographer. She talked to the people she wanted to photograph and tried to understand what their lives were like. Her photographs show poverty and hardship but also **resilience**. When government officials saw her images, they sent food and other supplies to help people in need.

"Migrant Mother"

During the Second World War, Japan fought against the United States. The USA government believed that Japanese Americans were a danger to the country and imprisoned them in camps. In 1942, the USA government hired Dorothea to take photographs to document the relocation of these families. No one got to see the photographs until many years after the war – the army didn't allow Dorothea to publish the images because they showed how poorly these families were treated.

Dorothea Lange made it her mission to photograph the truth – to inform people about what was happening to others and try to improve their lives. Many photographers followed Dorothea's lead, documenting the world around them and making sure no one would forget the events that shaped the world.

7 COMPOSERS

You might think a composer only writes classical music played by an orchestra, but *every* kind of music you listen to has been written by someone: pop music, rock music, hip-hop, rap. From the music you hear during a film, television show or advert, to a video game or the tune your computer makes when you turn it on, there's always a person who's thought about the sound and composed a tune. If you write music just for yourself, you're a composer too.

In the early 20th century, it was hard for women to make a living writing music; many women who had musical talent became teachers to earn money. It was even harder for Black women to be successful composers, but some recognised the challenges they faced due to racist attitudes, and persevered anyway. In 1926, Eva Jessye became the director of one of the first all-Black professional choirs in the USA.

As the century moved on, more women were being recognised for their music-writing talent. In the 1960s, musician and composer Delia Derbyshire changed the sound of orchestral music by using electronic sounds rather than instruments, and she was responsible for arranging the music to the BBC television programme *Dr Who*. By the end of the 20th century, British female composers were winning major awards for their work.

Delia Derbyshire at work

FLORENCE PRICE

Florence Price, who composed over 300 works, including **symphonies** and **concertos**, didn't let society's attitude towards her because of the colour of her skin, or the fact she was a woman, stop her from achieving success. Florence was born into a mixed-race family in 1887, and lived in Little Rock, Arkansas, USA. Her father, James, was African-American, and her mother, also called Florence, was White. James was the only Black dentist in the area and Florence was a schoolteacher and taught piano. Florence played the piano from a young age and her mother encouraged her to carry on with a musical education after high school.

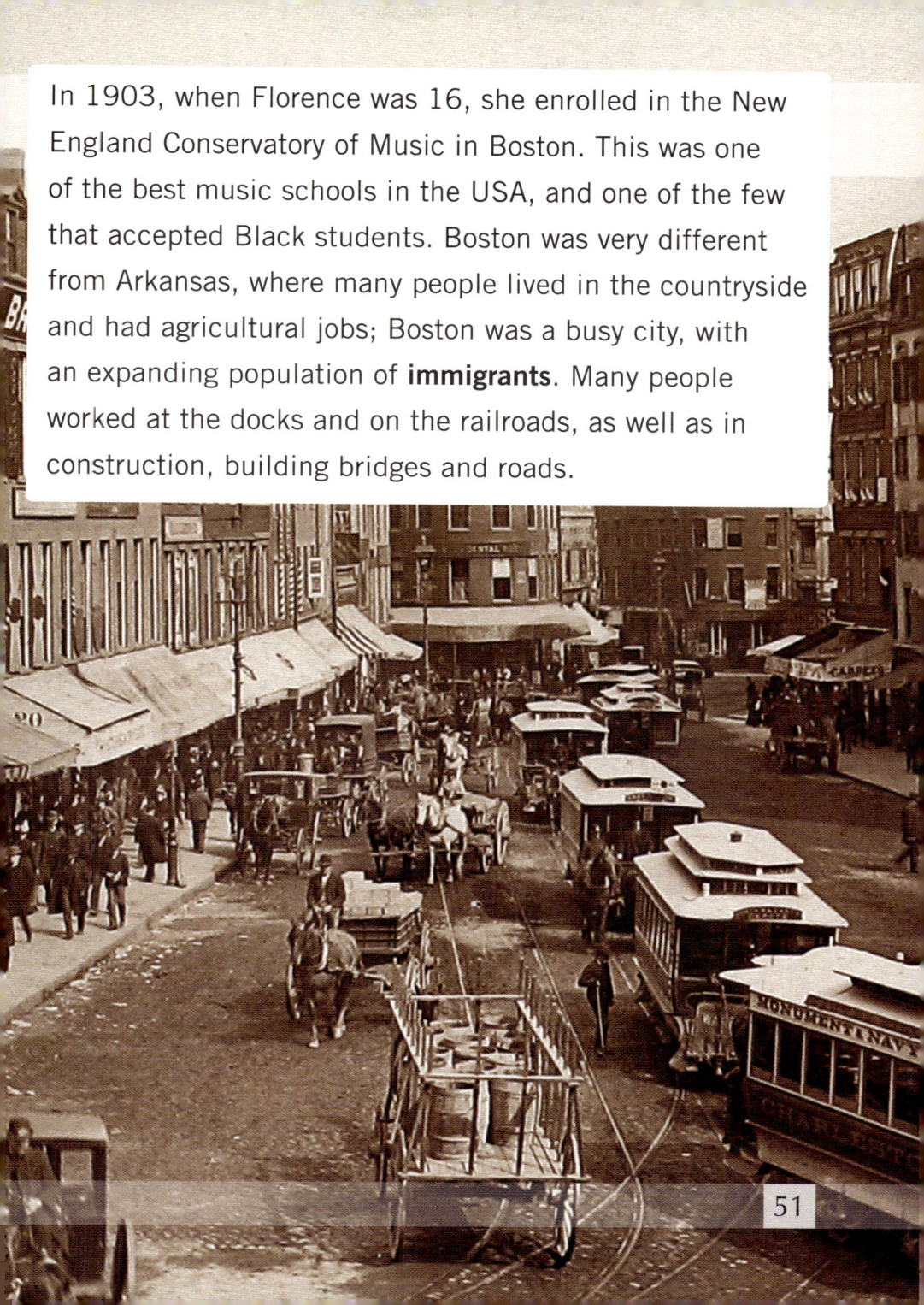

In 1903, when Florence was 16, she enrolled in the New England Conservatory of Music in Boston. This was one of the best music schools in the USA, and one of the few that accepted Black students. Boston was very different from Arkansas, where many people lived in the countryside and had agricultural jobs; Boston was a busy city, with an expanding population of **immigrants**. Many people worked at the docks and on the railroads, as well as in construction, building bridges and roads.

SEGREGATION

Florence studied the organ and the piano at the New England Conservatory and graduated with **honours**. By 1910, Florence had become the head of the Music Department at Clark Atlanta University, Georgia, but gave up work when she got married in 1912. Florence and her husband moved back to Little Rock and had two children, but Arkansas had changed.

In some southern states, there were laws enforcing racial segregation. When Florence was a child, these laws meant that Black children and White children couldn't go to the same school. By 1920, there were laws that Black people and White people had to be completely separated. Not everyone obeyed these laws in Arkansas, but Florence found it difficult to get a job.

Black people couldn't use the same facilities as White people.

In 1927, there was lots of unrest in Little Rock between the Black and White communities, and Florence and her family decided to move from Arkansas to Chicago. Florence had been studying **composition** and writing music for years and in 1928 she published four pieces of music for piano. Then, Florence and her husband divorced, so she had to get a job.

In 1931, Florence worked as an organist for silent film screenings. A film with sound was called a "talkie", and the first one was shown in the USA in 1927. However, many films were still silent – if you went to the cinema, you could watch images on the screen, but you couldn't hear the actors talking. The only sound would have been from musicians who played during the film.

Musicians at the front of the theatre, playing background music to the film.

53

In 1932, Florence entered one of her symphonies into a music competition. She used her classical training to combine African-American harmonies and folk songs into her music, and people liked it. Florence won first prize, and her symphony was performed by the Chicago Symphony Orchestra. She was the first African American to be recognised as a symphonic composer, and the music she composed was performed by other orchestras.

Florence was friends with many people in the art world; she was part of a network of Black people who helped and supported each other and their work. This group included the well-known writer Langston Hughes, and Florence set some of his poems to music. By the time Florence died in 1953, she was also well-known, but she left a secret.

REDISCOVERING FLORENCE

The house Florence used to live in was abandoned for many years. In 2009, nearly 60 years after Florence died, the couple who bought the house found dozens of manuscripts scattered on the floor. These were all unpublished works by Florence, that no one had known about. Some of the music that was discovered in her abandoned house has now been published and performed; Florence's music will live on.

Florence's abandoned house, St. Anne, Illinois.

8 CLASSICAL MUSICIANS

In 1898, the first women-only orchestra was founded in Berlin by the pianist, composer and conductor Mary Wurm. There were no professional orchestras with male *and* female musicians until 1913, when the Queen's Hall Orchestra in London hired six female violinists; by 1918, there were 14 female musicians.

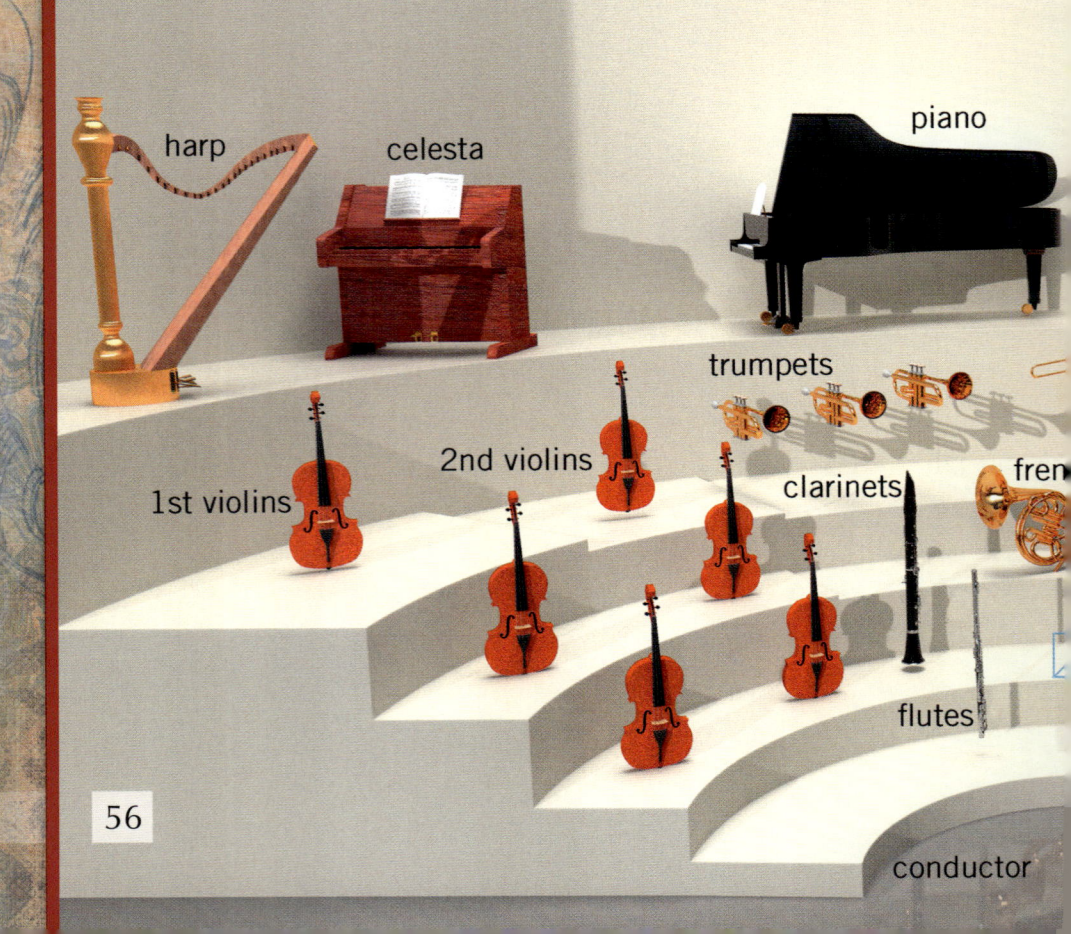

- harp
- celesta
- piano
- trumpets
- 1st violins
- 2nd violins
- clarinets
- fren[ch horn]
- flutes
- conductor

A woman playing violin, harp or flute was acceptable – these were seen as delicate, high-pitched instruments suitable for women. They couldn't play trombone, cello or double bass – these instruments were for men.

Pioneering female musicians in the 20th century proved that women could play any instrument in an orchestra, but this took time. In 1944, Maisie Ringham became the first woman to be a principal trombonist in a British orchestra. In 1966, Orin O'Brien became a permanent member of the New York Philharmonic Orchestra playing double bass.

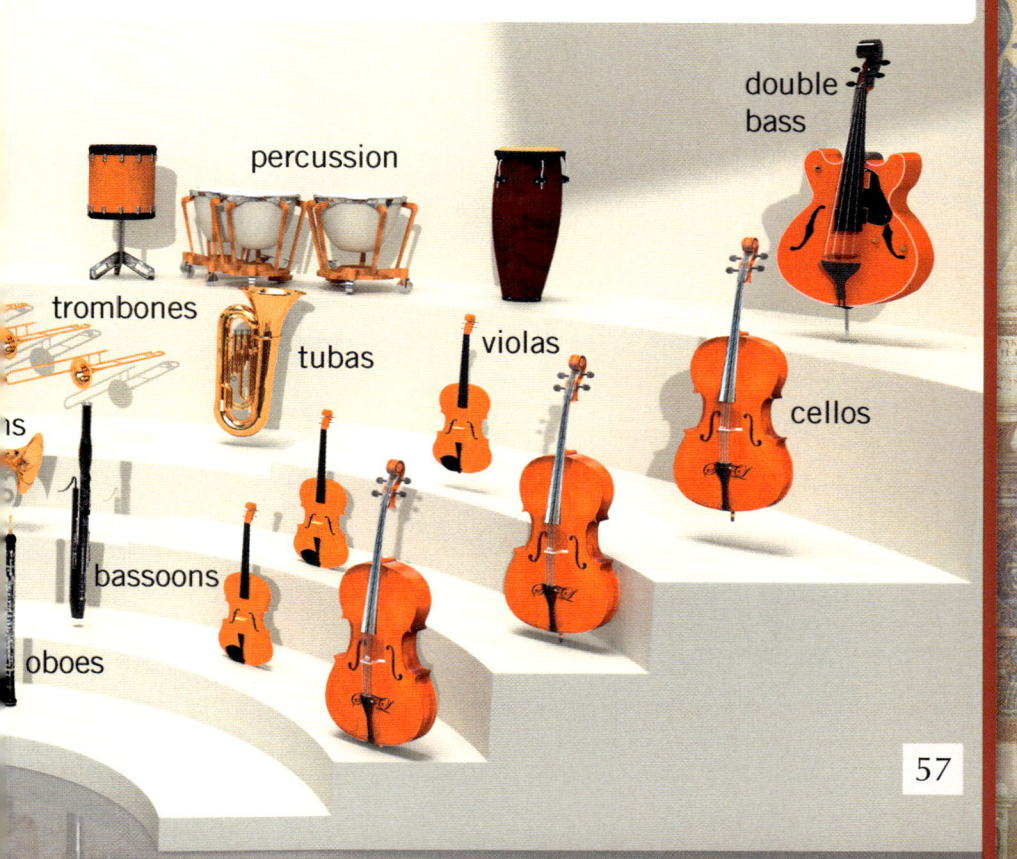

JACQUELINE DU PRÉ

Jacqueline du Pré became one of the 20th century's greatest cellists, and it was her mother, Iris, who noticed her early talent. Jacqueline was born in 1945, the year the Second World War ended. She and her family lived in Oxford, UK, where Jacqueline's mother was a professional pianist and music teacher. The du Pré household was a lively, musical one and one of Jacqueline's earliest memories is of listening to someone playing the cello on the radio. She asked her mother if she could play one too — she was just four.

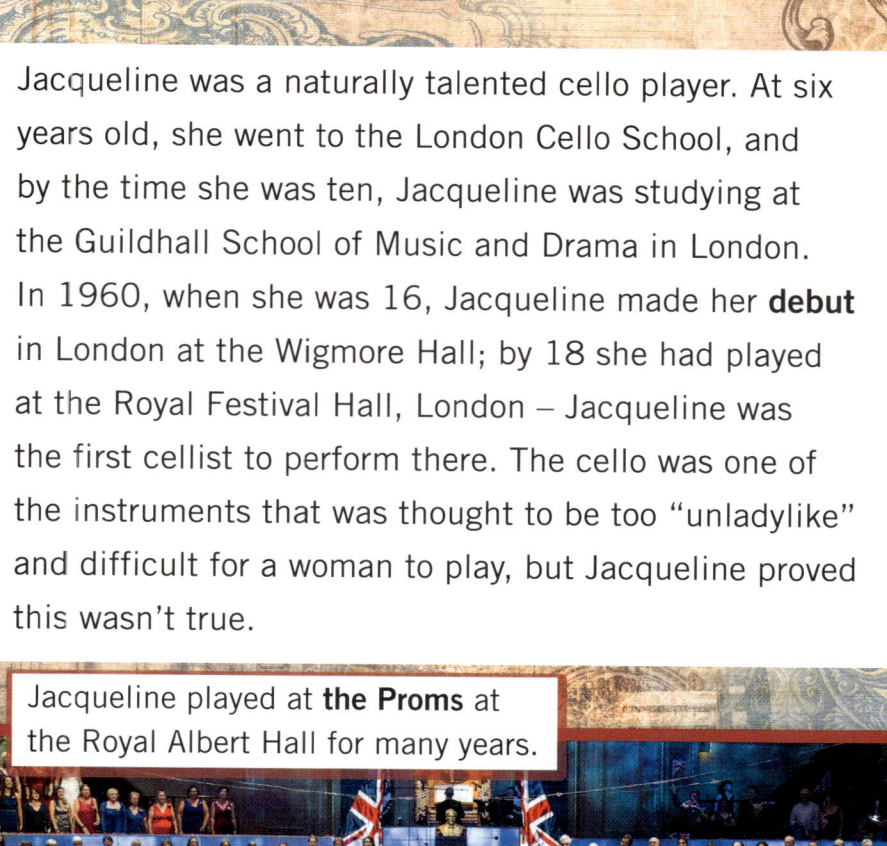

Jacqueline was a naturally talented cello player. At six years old, she went to the London Cello School, and by the time she was ten, Jacqueline was studying at the Guildhall School of Music and Drama in London. In 1960, when she was 16, Jacqueline made her **debut** in London at the Wigmore Hall; by 18 she had played at the Royal Festival Hall, London – Jacqueline was the first cellist to perform there. The cello was one of the instruments that was thought to be too "unladylike" and difficult for a woman to play, but Jacqueline proved this wasn't true.

Jacqueline played at **the Proms** at the Royal Albert Hall for many years.

THE RIGHT CELLO

When Jacqueline was 16, her godmother gave her a very special cello. It was over 200 years old, made by Antonio Stradivari. Antonio was an expert who built and repaired stringed instruments, including violins, guitars, harps and cellos. He lived in Cremona, Italy, in the 17th and 18th centuries and the instruments he designed are considered to be the very best. Antonio made over 70 cellos in his lifetime, and the instruments that still exist today are worth tens of millions of pounds.

Antonio Stradivari

In 1964, Jacqueline was given a second cello by her godmother – this was also made by Stradivari – and it was the instrument she used until the end of her career. In 1965, Jacqueline won a British Council scholarship to study in Russia with Mstislav Rostropovich, a world-class conductor, pianist and cellist. Jacqueline loved performing, particularly in front of an audience; she toured the USA in the same year and played with orchestras from around the world.

Jacqueline described her cello as her "best friend".

Jacqueline married classical pianist and conductor Daniel Barenboim in 1967. They were seen as a "golden couple" in the music world, and Jacqueline planned another tour of the USA. But just before one of her performances, Jacqueline's fingers went numb, and she found it difficult to lift her bow and move her fingers on the strings.

In 1973, when she was 28, Jacqueline was diagnosed with multiple sclerosis. Symptoms of multiple sclerosis include blurred vision, difficulty balancing, numbness or tingling in the body, and problems with memory. There's no cure and Jacqueline never played the cello in public again.

Jacqueline's diagnosis didn't mean the end of her career, it just looked different. She became a teacher and **mentor** to other young cello players, and in 1980, Jacqueline narrated a recording of the story *Peter and the Wolf*, accompanied by the English Chamber Orchestra. The orchestra was conducted by Jacqueline's husband, Daniel. Jacqueline died when she was 42, but recordings of her extraordinary playing still inspire musicians today.

In 1976, Jacqueline was awarded the Order of the British Empire (OBE).

9 FASHION DESIGNERS

In the early 1900s, dresses were long and covered most of the body; narrow waists were emphasised by corsets, which were worn under the dress. Silk, satin and chiffon were popular materials, usually in soft colours with decoration added. By the 1920s, dresses had a simpler, straighter shape; they were shorter in length but still had lots of decoration.

In the 1940s, after the Second World War, there was a shortage of material, but that didn't stop a new style emerging – dresses with pleated full skirts. This style was still popular in the 1950s, but then something new happened. Lots of different clothing designs became available; women could now choose from different styles, not just one.

In the 1960s, the mini-skirt was in! Designers like Mary Quant were inspired by Pop Art and used new materials like acrylic and polyester. By the 1960s and 1970s, ready-to-wear clothing was more accessible – instead of having to go to a dressmaker to make your clothing, you could go to a shop and buy something already made.

In the 1980s, people dressed in sportswear even when they weren't doing any sport. Women wore coloured suits with big shoulder pads. This was called "power dressing" and it was used to show someone had (or wanted to have) some authority. Evening dresses had big, puffed shoulders and large bows, but by the end of the century, fashion had become very relaxed and simple.

VIVIENNE WESTWOOD

Vivienne Westwood was born in 1941 in a tiny village called Tintwistle, Derbyshire, UK, where her father repaired shoes, and her mother worked at a cotton mill. In 1958, they relocated to Harrow, Middlesex, when Vivienne was 17. Vivienne worked at a local factory and then trained to become a primary school teacher, but the moment she met an art student called Malcolm McLaren, her life changed.

Vivienne and Malcolm ran a stall selling second-hand vintage clothing, and T-shirts Vivienne had **customised**. Vivienne liked clothes that were rebellious, that didn't look like the sort of outfits worn by older people, and she played a big part in creating a new style called "punk".

In the 1970s, punk fashion was worn by people who wanted to express themselves. If you dyed your hair bright, bold colours, had a mohawk style haircut, wore a dark leather jacket and some of your clothing was ripped, you were a punk!

mohawk hairstyle

FROM SHOP TO CATWALK

In 1971, Vivienne and Malcolm opened a small shop on the King's Road, London, and sold clothing that other high-street stores didn't sell. Vivienne wanted young people to be rebellious, just like the clothes she sold! Unfortunately, Vivienne was disappointed. Young people wore rebellious clothing, but she felt they weren't doing anything to change society.

Vivienne Westwood's shop on the King's Road, London.

Vivienne spent years teaching herself how to design and make clothes, and in 1981, Vivienne and Malcolm created their first clothing collection for a fashion show – and it was nothing like punk. These clothes were loose, striped and colourful; models wore large, patterned shirts with tasselled sashes and wide hats. They looked like highwaymen and women, and the collection was called Pirates.

PUTTING ON A SHOW

The Pirates show was just the beginning. Vivienne continued designing by herself and went on to create more collections of clothes; she worked on a sewing machine in her flat, and her designs were inspired by where she grew up in Derbyshire, the natural landscape and architecture. In the 1990s, Vivienne used details from historical paintings, and how women were dressed, and reinterpreted them in her own style. Dresses may have looked like those worn by women in the past, but they weren't. Vivienne designed corsets, but these were worn as a top, not underneath a dress.

Vivienne also designed platform shoes. In 1993, one model wearing the shoes at a fashion show found them so difficult to walk in, they fell over. This didn't stop people buying them.

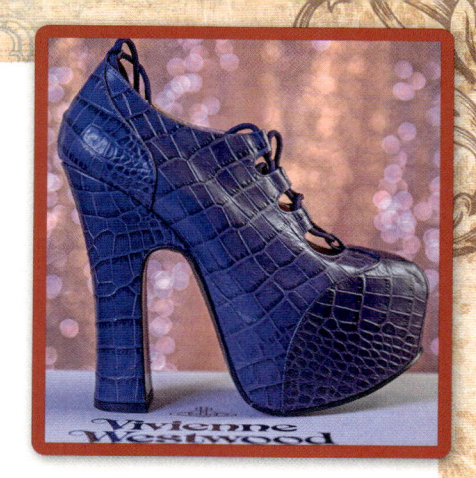

Moving into the 21st century, in 2004, the Victoria and Albert Museum, London, put on a show of Vivienne Westwood's designs. It was the largest exhibition the museum has ever had for a British designer.

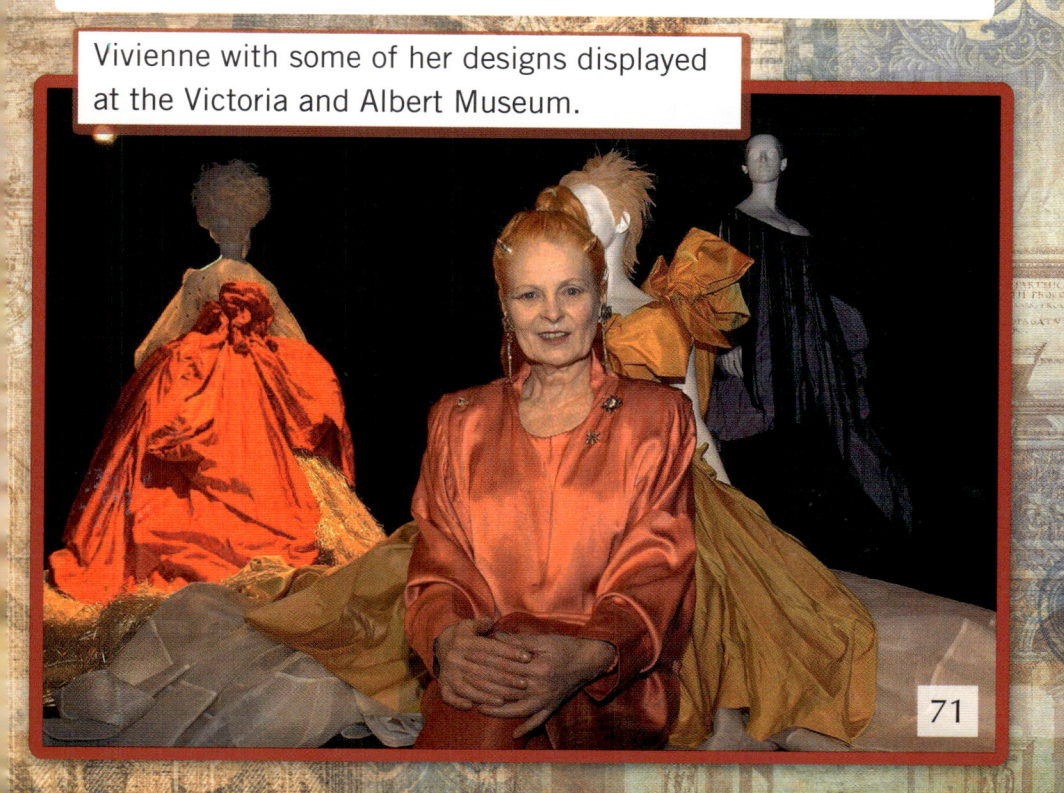

Vivienne with some of her designs displayed at the Victoria and Albert Museum.

ACTIVIST

Vivienne Westwood's success as a designer didn't stop her wanting to change the world. She created an organisation that fundraises for important causes such as halting climate change. Vivienne wanted people to be aware of what was happening around the globe; she was determined to stand up and make a difference and encourage others to do the same.

From the way Vivienne designed clothes to the causes she fought hard for – these were acts of rebellion – her way of making a difference and changing the world. This was recognised when Vivienne received a Lifetime Achievement Award for her significant contribution as a designer and for her continued fight to encourage people to take care of the planet.

Vivienne on a protest march: The People's March for Climate, Justice and Jobs, 2015

10 WHAT NEXT?

At the start of the 20th century, many creative people looked at the past, and decided they could do better! There were brand new sounds, the discovery of modern materials, innovative ways of working … and women changing the way things were done.

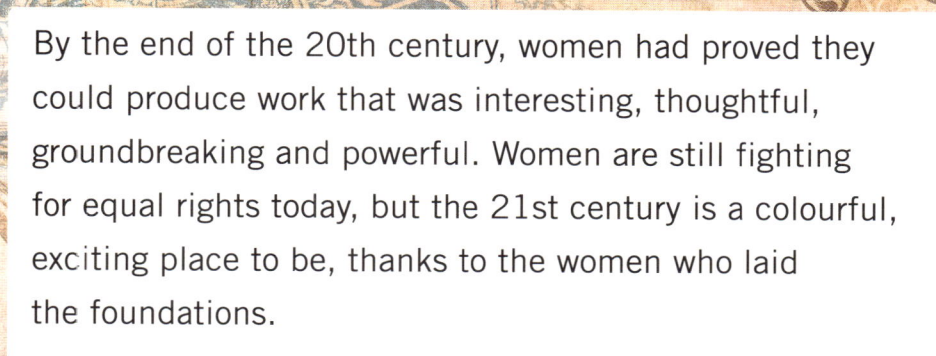

By the end of the 20th century, women had proved they could produce work that was interesting, thoughtful, groundbreaking and powerful. Women are still fighting for equal rights today, but the 21st century is a colourful, exciting place to be, thanks to the women who laid the foundations.

What will the next hundred years look like? Could you be one of the new generations of creative people producing something new? If you are, you might do something that makes a difference to people now … and in the future.

GLOSSARY

ancestral groups groups of people with a shared culture, traditions and history

composition the process of creating a piece of music

concertos music written for one, or a small group of musicians, to perform with an orchestra

conscription a law saying you have to fight

contemporary belonging to the present time

customised modified or changed something

cutting-edge latest or most advanced stage in the development of something

debut the first appearance in a particular role

discriminate make an unjust distinction in the treatment of different people

domestic worker someone paid to help clean a home

exile living away from where you come from, usually unwillingly

groundbreaking original and important

homesteads areas of land including a farmhouse and outbuildings

honours an academic achievement for someone who has done work of a high standard

immigrants people who come to a country to live there permanently

immunised to make someone resistant to diseases

mentor an experienced and trusted adviser

ochre light yellow, brown or red colour made from natural things like mud and plants

paralysis loss of ability to move, and sometimes to feel, in part of the body

preserve keep something in its original state

Proms, the a classical music festival, which takes place every year in London

resilience the ability to withstand or recover from something difficult

sacred an important place or object, which people respect

symphonies carefully arranged music written for a full orchestra

United Nations an international organisation where people meet to discuss common problems

INDEX

Abstract Expressionism 17
apartheid 35, 37, 39
Art Deco 25
Cubism 16
disco music 33
documentary photography 46
electronic dance music 33
Expressionism 16
First World War 4, 16, 24
Great Depression 44–45
hip-hop music 48
Jazz 32, 36

Minimalism 17
Modernism 25
Pop Art 17, 65
pop music 6, 48
punk 67, 69
rap 48
rock and roll /rock music 6, 33, 48
Second World War 5, 8, 11, 12, 17, 24, 40, 47, 58, 64
segregation 52
suffragette 3
Surrealism 16

100 YEARS

ARCHITECTS

CLASSICAL MUSICIANS

COMPOSERS

PHOTOGRAPHERS

78

WRITERS

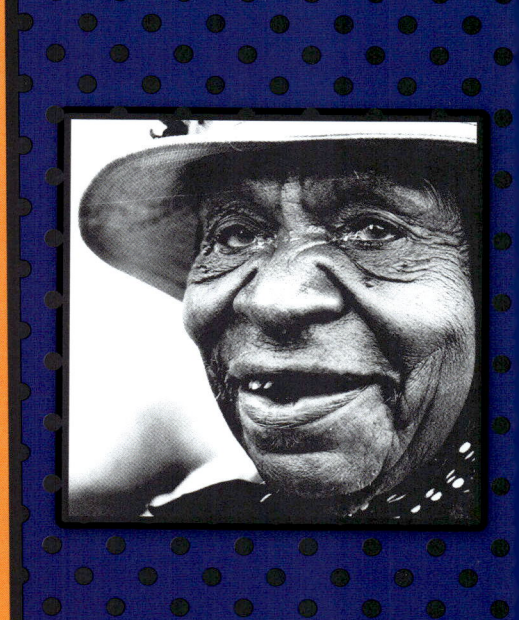

PAINTERS

FASHION DESIGNERS

SINGERS

Ideas for reading

Written by Gill Matthews
Primary Literacy Consultant

Reading objectives:
- check that the book makes sense to them, discussing their understanding and exploring the meaning of words in context
- retrieve, record and present information from non-fiction
- participate in discussions about books that are read to them and those they can read for themselves, building on their own and others' ideas and challenging views courteously

Spoken language objectives:
- use relevant strategies to build their vocabulary
- articulate and justify answers, arguments and opinions
- participate in discussions, presentations, performances, role play, improvisations and debates

Curriculum links: History: a study of an aspect or theme in British history that extends pupils' chronological knowledge beyond 1066

Interest words: rights, suffragette, campaigned, governing, deeds

Build a context for reading

- Ask children to look at the front cover of the book and to read the title. Explore what the title means to them. Ask what they think the book might be about.
- Read the back-cover blurb. Ask how this helps them to predict what they might find out from the book.
- Point out that this is an information book. Ask children to explain what features are typically found in a non-fiction book and to elaborate on the organisation and purpose of the features. Give them time to skim the book looking for the features they have named.
- Read pp2–7 aloud. Discuss with the children how they feel about the information they have been given. Encourage them to support their responses with reasons and evidence from the text.
- Challenge children to find the words in bold in this chapter and to try to work out their meanings from the context before checking in the glossary.